Linux for Beginner's

Complete Guide for Linux Operating System and Command Line

By Terence Lawfield

Published in Canada

© Copyright 2015 – Terence Lawfield

ISBN-13: 978-1511473736
ISBN-10: 1511473738

Table of Contents

Introduction

Linux has been around for a long time, although many people have never even heard of it. Despite this, the operating system is found in cars, smartphones, and even household appliances. Yes, Linux is practically all around you in your daily life. It is little wonder that people are becoming increasingly interested in learning how to use this versatile, free, and opensource operating system on their own computers.

What is Linux?

While it certainly isn't an operating system that the public think of, when they think about computers — it is extremely popular. With relatively little exposure in the media, and a group of common misconceptions turning people away from using Linux, it is still regarded as a great operating system.

If you use a computer already, you are almost certainly using an operating systems. They are basically collections of computer programs that allow you to use your computer. Without one of these, people would have no way to interact with their computers.

The most commonly used operating systems on home computers are Windows and Mac OS. However, Linux is an operating system that many people choose to use instead.

Chapter 1:
What to Expect From
This Book

If you are looking for an advanced guide to using every single aspect of Linus — this is the wrong book for you. This is an easy-to-follow guide for people who are still beginners at using Linux, as well as those who have never used it in their lives, or do not even have it yet.

In this book, you will be taken through all of the basics, including obtaining your copy of Linux, testing it out to see if you would like to use it, installing the full version, and how to go about doing all of the basic tasks in Linux. You will also learn some basics about the command line, but you can skim that part for now, if you choose.

Chapter 2:
Brief History of Linux

You could be forgiven for thinking that Linux is new, but it has actually been around since the beginning of the 1990s. While it was very different to forms of Linux that people primarily use today, the early versions built the foundation for what was to come.

Here is a brief time line of the history of Linux:

1970s: Unix was released, after being developed at the end of the previous decade. It was mainly used for academic and business purposes at this time.

1983: Richard Stallman, a computer programmer, started the GNU Project. His goal was to make an operating system similar to Unix, with only free software.

1987: Andrew Tanenbaum made Minix, which was similar to Unix, and aimed at academic users.

1991: Linus Torvalds, a student from Finland, created a

free version of Minix — which he named Linux. This title was a combination of "Minix" and his own first name.

After Linux was first created, it has steadily evolved, with many different versions, leading up until this very day.

Chapter 3:
Why Choose Linux?

If you are reading this book, you either have Linux and need some help learning how to use it, or you are thinking about getting Linux. For those who are still "on the fence" about making the switch to this operating system, this section should help you decide.

One problem with technology fanatics is that they can be very biased — almost like sports fans. If you were to speak with someone who loves Linux, and has been using it for years, they might paint a very positive picture of it. In addition, they would probably tell you that the other operating systems are junk. However, someone who loves Mac OS or Windows might inform you that Linux is junk, and that you shouldn't bother trying to use it.

Many people seem to believe that Linux is overly complicated, and that only truly dedicated tech-lovers could ever hope to figure out how to use it. That is very untrue, and if you are worried that Linux is hard to use, leave those thoughts behind. There are versions of Linux that many believe are more user-friendly than anything else available.

Now, with an open mind, take a look at some of the top reasons why you should choose to use Linux:

It is *free*. This is probably one of the biggest reasons for many people to choose anything. Of course, your computer probably came with an operating system already, and that would make this a minor factor. Have you thought about updates in the future? It will cost money to upgrade to the latest operating systems, in most situations. On the other hand, Linux is free and it will almost certainly be free long into the future.

Great with slow computers. Many people choose to install Linux on older, slower computers. If you are still using an old PC from 10 years ago, the chances are that it will not run a new operating system well. Many people are happy running the operating system that came with their old computer. However, in time, these stop being supported, making them very unsecure, and almost impossible to use in any productive way.

There are some versions of Linux that are specifically designed to run on low-end hardware, so you can get more out of your old PC.

But keep in mind that not all versions of Linux will run well on slower hardware.

Greater security. If you have been online much in your life, you are probably painfully aware of computer viruses. Even if you do have an antivirus on other computers, there is still a chance that your system with be corrupted. Linux users do not have to worry about computer viruses. In fact, you will not even need to install an antivirus on a computer running Linux.

Easy to use. Back in the early days of Linux, it certainly was a complicated system to use. However, that was quite some time ago, and things have greatly changed. Many people think that Linux is only for the truly "nerdy", who know a lot about computers. That is far from the truth these days, and many versions of Linux are simple, with attractive interfaces, and lots of automation.

No need to find drivers. When you use a new piece of hardware, you will generally need a driver. This is a piece of software that tells your computer *how* to use your new piece of hardware, like a new printer, for example. With Linux, practically everything is plug-and-play. Just make sure that your hardware is all supported, as mentioned earlier in this chapter.

The software repository. Think of this like the Linux "app store". You don't need to look around online, or worry about installing things manually, because Linux has you covered. In addition, software that you find in the repository will be compatible with your version of Linux, safe to use, and always updated automatically.

Updates are painless. Updates are often the bane of people's computer using existence. If you have ever tried to use your computer, only to find that an automatic update has taken over — you will appreciate the ease of Linux updates. They are simply installed in the background, quickly and easily. You will not need to wait to shut down your computer either.

Attractive GUI. The GUIs (Graphical User Interfaces) of some versions of Linux are just beautiful. These include Unity, Gnome, and KDE, to name just a few. In comparison, Windows — and even Mac OS — can often seem boring and even ugly. In addition to this, it's possible to customize just how your interface looks, in many ways.

If you are happy with your current operating system, you might have no good reasons to change over. However, if there are things that regularly bother you, it might be time to take a closer look at swapping over to Linux.

Chapter 4:
Why Avoid Linux?

Obviously, Linux is not ideal for everyone. While it is considered a great choice for many, there are still some who would be better off sticking with Windows or Mac OS.

Here are some of the reasons that you might want to avoid installing Linux:

You love gaming. Most Linux lovers will not deny that it is harder to find games for their operating system of choice. If you are into gaming on your computer, Windows is still the best option.

You rely on a specific piece of software. This is probably one of the main reasons for people to stick with an operating system they know.

While the choice of software on Linux is expanding, there are still many popular programs that simply are not available for it. If you need a certain program, especially for work, you might want to avoid using Linux.

Your PC's hardware isn't supported. Many hardware manufacturers do not offer driver support for new products. This means that you might not be able to use Linux with everything on your computer yet, although this is an increasingly uncommon problem.

Chapter 5:
Getting Started

What are Distributions

There are many different versions of Linux, as we discussed earlier. They have been developed for many reasons, by many people. You should be able to find something that suits your particular needs, no matter what you use your computer for. Think of the different Linux distributions as various "flavors", with each one a little different, but still essentially the same thing, at a foundation level at least.

Just about all of the different Linux distributions are available for free, and can be downloaded readily. In addition to this, since most of the distributions are freeware, it is completely legal to copy them, burn them to CD, DVD, USB drives, and give them to people you know.

Choosing Your Distribution

This is one of the areas where a lot of people become stuck. Unlike with Windows and Mac OS, you will have to make a choice about which version to use. Distrowatch is a website that lists the distributions that are currently most popular, with details about them.

There are a number of different user interfaces, which are basically all of the visuals that you will see, like menus and icons. Ubuntu uses Unity, which is a very stylistic and easy-to-use interface, much like Mac OS. There are also more traditional looking desktop interfaces, like KDE, which somewhat resembles Windows XP.

If you are just starting, it's best to choose a popular version of Linux. That way, there will be plenty of information about it, and it should be relatively easy for you to find help.

Before you choose a Linux distribution, ask yourself these questions:

- Are you very good with a computer?
- Do you like a stylish, modern desktop, or a more traditional one?
- Is your computer very powerful?

If you have fairly basic computer skills, Ubuntu, Linux Mint, or Deepin are your best bets. If you consider that your computer skills are moderately good, Fedora or Debian are also good choices. For advanced users, there are other options — but this is a book for beginners, so these will not be covered.

If your computer is reasonably powerful, Ubuntu with Unity is highly recommended. It is easy to use, and has a huge community of users.

If you are using an older computer, or one that is pretty slow, Xubuntu is a great choice. It is a more traditional looking version of Ubuntu, which uses a less power-hungry interface, but you can still use the same software as with regular Ubuntu.

Try Linux First

Your computer probably already has an operating system running, and you might not want to delete it just yet. That is fine, because you can actually try Linux without deleting your old operating system. This is done using a Live distribution. With one of these, you can run Linux from a USB drive, CD, or DVD. It will not change anything on your computer's hard drive either, so there is no real risk in giving Linux a go. After you have finished trying Linux, you can choose to just stop using the Live distribution, or you can install Linux properly.

To get a Live distribution running, go to the Linux Live USB Creator website and download it. Once you have done this, follow the simply instructions in the help section of this website. You will need a USB drive (also knows as a flash drive or USB stick). It will give you the option of choosing the distribution that you want, from a range of different choices. If you are not sure about which options to choose, go with the defaults and start the creation of your Live distribution. Don't worry, because you can easily delete this from your USB drive. Once you have finished the process, you can run Linux from your new Live distribution USB drive, and it will work just like a regular Linux installation. See what you think, and you can use it to help you follow the rest of this guide.

This guide recommends that you download Ubuntu, and will primarily use this distribution for examples. Keep in mind that you will lose the changes you made to your Live distribution, when you finally install Linux fully.

Installing Linux

If you are like most people, you probably purchased your computer with an operating system already installed. There is a good chance that it came with Windows installed, or Mac OS if you purchased an Apple computer. The thought of installing your own operating system might seem like an extremely daunting task. Do not start to panic, because Linux is relatively simple to install.

After you have tested out the Live distribution, as detailed in the previous section, you might decide to install Linux properly.

To install Linux, once you have decided that you like it, follow these simple steps:

- This particular method will wipe your hard drive. Back up any files that you would like to keep, with a storage device, such as a portable hard drive, CDs, or DVDs.

- Find the option in your Live USB drive to install Linux and press it.

- Ensure that that your computer has the minimum requirements for the installation, and then continue.

- If you want to install updates and additional software, you will need an Internet connection. We will assume that you have access to the Internet for now. If you don't right now, you will need to do these things later.

- You will be asked how much of your hard drive space you want to allocate to different things. It is possible to install Linux side-by-side with another operating system, but this is a more advanced process. Remember, for the purposes of this guide, you will be completely wiping the hard drive, and freshly installing Linux. Make your selection, and begin the installation process.

- You will be given some set-up options, like choosing your location, the type of keyboard layout that you use, and some standard user options. Enter your choices and then you are ready to go. The system will finish the installation, and you will now have Linux on your computer.

Logging In

When you start up your computer, you might be logged in automatically. Otherwise, you will be faced with the login screen. This screen will be different for various versions of Linux, and you will be able to change how you want them to act.

You will be asked for your user name, which you selected during the installation process. After this, you will need to enter your password, to prove that you are in fact the owner of this user name. The login screens will usually have some other items, like the system's name, a clock, and options to restart or shut down your computer.

How to Get Software

Applications are even easier to install than the operating system, especially if you use the software repository that comes with Linux. As mentioned briefly, this is basically like an "app store", as you will find on Windows, Mac OS, iOS, and Android devices. If you have ever been unsure when look for the "right" software, or you worry about security risks — the software repositories will make life much simpler. On Ubuntu, it is called the Ubuntu Software Center, but other distributions of Linux will have varied names for it.

Software repositories are visually based, and you simply need to look through the categories, or perform a search, and then choose to install different software.

In order to install software using the command line in Ubuntu or Debian-based distributions, it is also fairly simple. If you like, you can skip to the next chapter, as this part is more advanced. The command for installing software in this manner is:

"sudo apt-get install [enter name of software]"

You will be asked for your user password, so enter it and press enter. The installation will begin, and that's all there is to it.

But what does this all mean? "Sudo" indicated that you have admin privileges, which you will need to install software. Avoid using this privileged commands when you do not need to, because you can accidentally cause changes that might damage your system.

If you are using a Fedora-based distribution, you would type:

"su yum install [enter name of software]"

Installing software on Linux, even if in the command line, is really simple. In fact, many would agree that it is easier than the installation process on other operating systems, where you are required to track down the right pieces of software, and then install them in a variety of ways.

Chapter 6:
The Linux Desktop

Now that you have Linux running on your computer, you will want to learn the basics. If you are coming from Windows or Mac OS, things will look different, but don't become discouraged. You have already learned how to install new software, so make sure that you find everything you need. Once you are happy with your selection of software, let's start to explore the rest of Linux.

When you have logged in, you will be shown the desktop, much like with Windows and Mac OS. This is your primary working area. In Ubuntu 10.10, there will be a panel across the top, as well as one on the bottom of the screen. Just like with other graphical operating systems, you will move the cursor around with your mouse, and click on icons to activate them. See, it's not that different, is it?

Desktop Panels

The bars on the top and bottom of the screen are panels, but you can customize your panels in a huge number of ways. By doing this, you can essentially create the Linux experience that perfectly suits your needs. For many, this is not needed, so don't feel obliged to experiment with your panels. If you like the default experience, that is all you need to use.

Your panels provide a place for you to start, when interacting with the desktop environment. They also give you various pieces of information about your computer. Notifications will appear on your panels as well. If you like, you can place your panels on the sides of the screen, by accessing the properties of your system.

Accessibility Options

If you need special accessibility options, like larger icons, or an on-screen keyboard, there will be an icon to access these. It is different for various systems; it looks like an illustration of a person inside a circle for some. Clicking on this icon will take you to a list of options, such as turning on a screen reader, magnifying glass, changing the colors in contrast, sticky keys, ignoring duplicate key presses, and pressing and holding keys.

Navigation

In order to move around inside your system, and access various files and software, you will need to learn how to navigate Linux. This sounds more difficult than it actually is. While different versions of Linux vary in how they deal with navigation, the process is pretty easy to pick up. If you click on your system settings, you will be taken to a list of options. Clicking on an option will take you to more options, etc., until you arrive where you want to go. This is basically all navigating is, and you can think of it like moving through chapters of a book. The main menus are like tables of contents, and they will show you the more detailed sections of each part of your computer system.

If you are used to using Windows or Mac OS, it should not take you long to figure out how to navigate through your computer. If you cannot find something, simply perform a search, and type in what you want to find. Ubuntu is especially powerful in this respect, as you can access a system, and online, search by using the Windows key on your keyboard.

Chapter 7:
Command Line

Command line is based on text, unlike the GUIs (graphical user interfaces) that people generally use these days. However, it can often be must simpler to use command line, especially when you want to get something done quickly. Do you remember the old days when Microsoft DOS was popular? You might recall seeing people working on computers, using nothing but text commands to get things done. That is what Linux command line does. There are different pieces of software for command line, and distributions will have their own versions. You can also install your own choice of command line application.

The very thought of using command line scares a lot of people, and they have no desire to do so. However, since you are reading this section, let's assume that you want to learn about command line, and begin with some basic commands. One great thing about working with command line is that you can work with a range of different Linux distributions, and always be able to do things the same way, with command line. Another reason that people like using command line is the pure power it gives them, although it is a little more complex to learn than graphical user interfaces.

Open up your command line software, which is also knows as your system's shell. This is called Terminal in Ubuntu, and you can find your shell with a quick system search. The keyboard shortcut to access Terminal is Ctrl + Alt + T, and this shortcut is the same for many versions of Linux.

Sudo

While learning to install software, you learned about the sudo command. You will need to enter this at the start of some commands, where admin privilege is required, but you should not use sudo for ordinary commands.

File and Directory Commands

In order to access different parts of your system, you will need to look at directories, and the files they contain. Directories are the folders of your system, containing files, and more folders with files, etc.

Here is a list of commands that will help you to navigate your files and directories:

"~" indicates your home directory, such as /home or /home/user (with your user name in the place of user).

"ls" This will display a list of the files in the directory that you are currently looking at.

"pwd" means "print working directory" and will tell you which directory you are currently in.

"cd" will let you "change directory", so that you can move around to different parts of your system.

If you type "cd /" you will be taken to your root, or base-level directory, so that's a good starting point if you become lost.

"cd" and "cd ~" are two commands that will take you to your home directory.

"cd .." Will go back up one directory.

"cd -" will simply go back to the previous directory that you were in.

You don't have to go through one directory at a time, if you know where you want to navigate. Let's say that you want to go to your "Documents" directory, which is located in a directory called "My Stuff". This might involve the command, "cd /my stuff/documents".

If you want to copy a file, use "cp" by entering "cp file mine /directory" where "mine" is the name of the file that you wish to copy, and "directory" is where you want to copy the file to. You can copy a directory in the same way, with the command "cp -r directory mine" where "mine" is a directory instead of a file.

If you want to move a file (as with cut & paste), use the "mv" command instead of "cp".

To delete a file, use "rm" with the name of the file, where "rm" stands for remove.

To delete an empty directory, use "rmdir".

To delete a directory, as well as anything that is inside, including directories and files, use "rm -r"

Create a new directory with the command "mkdir".

"man" will show you a manual of commands. If you want a manual of the types of manuals, you can enter "man man".

Those are the basics of navigating files and directories with command line, as well as moving them around. In a graphical interface, these are similar to dragging, dropping, cutting, and pasting files and folders, as well as simply clicking into different folders.

Running Files

Now that you have an idea of how to move around in your system, using the command line, it's time to run some files. It's pretty simple, and you can do it with this command:

"./nameoffile.extension"

In this example, "nameoffile" is the name of the file that you want to run, while ".extension" is the extension of the file. If you wanted to run text document called "story", you would type "./story.txt", as ".txt" is the correct extension for text files.

Firstly, you will need to go to the directory that contains the file, as discussed in the previous section. Remember that you can "ls" (list) the files in a directory, to make sure that it contains the one that you want to run.

If this is becoming too complex for you to understand, don't worry. You can always go back to using the graphical interface when you become stuck, and keep practicing with the command line in your own time.

System Commands

If you want to find out some information about your system, you can do that using command line as well. Here is a list of system information commands:

To find out how much space has been used on your disks, use "df -h". There are other ways to do this, but the "h" here stands for "human readable", and it will display the information in megabytes.

Use the command "du" to find out how much space a particular directory is using. This will show you information for all files, and directories, inside a directory. If you would rather an overview of the space used, the command "du -sh" will do this (with "s" meaning "summary" and "h" once again meaning "human readable").

To look at the total amounts of both used and free memory on your computer system, use the "free" command. To see this in megabytes, use the command "free -m".

To see an overview of the processes that are running on your system, use the "top" command (which stands for "table of processes"). After you have finished looking at your table of processes, you will need to press "q" to exit.

To get an overview of all system information, use the command "uname -a".

If you want information about the Linux distribution that you are currently running, use the command "lsb_release -a".

To see information about your networks, use the command "ip addr".

Adding New Users

You have already set up your own login details, but you can also add new users to your system. This is helpful if there will be more than one person using your computer.

To create a new user on your computer, use the following command:

- "adduser newuser", where "newuser" will be the user name of the person that you are adding. You can make this whatever you like.
- "passwd newuser" will let you give your new user a password.

Using Options

You can add options to your commands, and some of the commands listed have shown you how to do this. If you were to use the command "ls -s", that would use the "ls" command for listing the contents of a directory, with the "-s" option for adding file sizes as well. Another common option is the "-h" command, that you have already looked at, which makes the sizes "human readable".

If you were to type "ls -sh", you would be asking for a listing of the contents of a directory, and adding the options to show the sizes of everything, as well as displaying those sizes in megabytes, instead of blocks.

Keyboard Shortcuts

If you want to do something in Linux, and you use your graphical interface to look online for help, you will often find command line text that you can use. You don't need to understand anything about using these commands, and you can still benefit from them. You will need to copy the text, by highlighting it with your mouse in a normal fashion. However, if you try to use the common keyboard shortcut "Ctrl + V" to paste into the command line shell, it will not work. To paste text with command line, press "Ctrl + Shift + V" instead.

Using command line might seem like an awful lot of typing, but there are more keyboard shortcuts that you can use to save time:

Down arrow (or Ctrl + N): go back to your previous command.

Up arrow (or Ctrl + P): go through your previous commands.

Enter: *enter* the command, once you have found what you are looking for, or you have typed what you want.

Tab: will automatically complete file names and commands. If there is more than one option, it will give you a list to choose from.

Ctrl + R: will let you search through the commands that you have already entered. This is extremely useful for when you have entered some long commands. Simply use this keyboard shortcut, and then type part of the command that you want. It will then display commands that start with the text you have entered. Press Enter when you have found what you are looking for.

"History": entering this command will display a history of every command that you have used, next to a number. If there are too many commands to display, use the command "history | less" to give you a list that you can scroll through.

Chapter 8:
Popular Linux Software

If you are going to start using Linux, one of the first things that you will need is a good selection of software. In fact, many people stick with operating systems they hate, simply because they are hesitant to give up their favorite applications. All of the software listed below is completely free, and free to distribute to your friends or family. That should help to convince you that using Linux is a great idea.

You can actually run Windows software in Linux, using a program called Wine. However, you will basically be making your computer pretend to be using Windows. If you would prefer to use dedicated, and often more reliable, methods — you are going to need some great Linux software.

Microsoft Word Alternatives

One of the most widely used tools in the business world is Microsoft Office. Not long ago, if you were to apply for an office job without any knowledge of MS Office, you just might be laughed out of the room. This might still be the case in many companies. However, the days when MS Office was the one-and-only office suit are in the past.

Here are some great alternatives for Microsoft Office that run on Linux:

OpenOffice. This wonderful, free, opensource office suit runs on Linux, Windows, and Mac OS. Consequently, you will find many people who use it, and it is largely compatible with MS Office documents. You don't have to install the entire suite, but it contains software for word processing, spreadsheets, graphics, presentations, and databases. If you just want something that will let you get on with your office work, and you only want to try *one* office suit for Linux — make it OpenOffice.

LibreOffice. This one is based off OpenOffice, but the two makers separated in 2010. It is a little less feature-rich than OpenOffice, but will run better on slower machines. That makes it a great choice for businesses using old computers. Because of the small file size of LibreOffice, it can be installed to a USB drive, and used on different computers.

Google Docs. This is a very popular, online office suit, that ties in nicely with the rest of Google's online products. If you already use a Google account, you will not need to do anything but sign in. You can change your settings to be able to work offline, via your Internet browser, so Google Docs is no longer "online only".

Internet Browsers

If you are using a computer these days, you probably need to be online, in order to be productive. Luckily, you have plenty of choices for Linux web browsers. You can even use the most popular browsers in Linux, so you won't have to settle for something else.

Here are some great Linux web browsers that you can try:

Firefox. This is one of the most popular web browsers for Linux users. There are faster options out there, as well as newer ones, but Firefox is considered one of the best.

Chrome. You will need to download this from Google, as it won't be in the software repositories. However, you can use Chromium instead, if you insist on using the repositories. This is the number one web browser at the moment, and you will glad to know that Google fully supports Chrome for Linux.

In-built browsers. Whatever version of Linux you choose, it will almost definitely come with a web browser, and that might even be Firefox or Chromium. If you are not fussy about what you use, and just need to check websites every now-and-then, you might be happy to use a default browser.

Audio, Video, and Image

If you want to be able to manipulate media files, whether creating a piece of art, recording a song, trimming down the video of your latest vacation, or just watching it — Linux has some create choices on offer.

GIMP. If you want something to replace Photoshop, this is your best choice. However, there are some places where GIMP simply isn't as good.

PiTiVi. If you want to do some basic home movie editing, this is a great choice of software. While it will not give you the more professional functionality of Final Cut Pro, there are plenty of functions to choose from.

Audacity. When it comes to working with sound files, this is the go-to application for Linux users. With it, you can record multi-track audio files, cut them up, rearrange them, and add effects.

VLC. This is a popular media player that is both powerful and reliable. It will let you play more types of files than just about any other media player.

Email Clients

If you need your computer for work, you will probably want a good email client. Windows users will probably be familiar with Outlook, but there are some good alternatives for Linux.

Thunderbird. This is made by Mozilla, the same company that brought you Firefox. It is a lightweight, easy-to-use email client, with lots of different options.

KMail. This is the default for KDE desktop environments. It has loads of features, although you might take a bit of time to get used to its layout.

Evolution. This generally comes with the GNOME desktop environment. It will let you use Google Calendar right away, as well as Microsoft Exchange. It looks good, and is simple to use.

Instant Messages

If you are used to staying in touch with people on your computer, it's important to keep that functionality when you swap over to Linux. Here are some good IM applications that you can try:

Skype. This is an extremely popular instant messenger, and many people would be unwilling to part with using it.

Pidgin. This IM software has been around for a long time, and lets you log onto Facebook, Yahoo, Google, and many other networks.

Conclusion

As you have already experienced, the world of Linux is vast and seemingly goes on forever. It is understandable for people to feel daunted by the idea of swapping over to using Linux, just because there are so many options. However, if you choose a popular distribution, like Ubuntu, and choose from the software listed in this book, you have nothing to worry about.

If you are the type of person who loves to have options, and wants to be able to tweak your operating system to your heart's content — Linux just might be the most fun that you have ever had sitting at your computer.

You have entered a wonderful world, where you have the freedom to choose how you use your computer. There is a massive community of Linux users on the Internet, and they are generally friendly and helpful. The next step is yours to make: are you willing to finally start using Linux, and leave Windows and Mac OS behind?

DISCLAIMER AND/OR LEGAL NOTICES: Every effort has been made to accurately represent this book and it's potential. Results vary with every individual, and your results may or may not be different from those depicted. No promises, guarantees or warranties, whether stated or implied, have been made that you will produce any specific result from this book. Your efforts are individual and unique, and may vary from those shown. Your success depends on your efforts, background and motivation.

The material in this publication is provided for educational and informational purposes only and is not intended as medical advice. The information contained in this book should not be used to diagnose or treat any illness, metabolic disorder, disease or health problem. Always consult your physician or health care provider before beginning any nutrition or exercise program. Use of the programs, advice, and information contained in this book is at the sole choice and risk of the reader.